AF498046

COURS GRADUÉ

DE

VERSIONS ANGLAISES

COURS GRADUÉ

DE

VERSIONS ANGLAISES

Choisies dans les Ouvrages indiqués par les Programmes officiels

A L'USAGE DES CLASSES MOYENNES

PAR

M. l'abbé MOUSSEIGNE

LICENCIÉ ÈS LETTRES

PROFESSEUR D'ANGLAIS AU PETIT-SÉMINAIRE DE SAINT-PÉ

DELHOMME ET BRIGUET, ÉDITEURS

LYON	PARIS
3, AVENUE DE L'ARCHEVÊCHÉ, 3	83, RUE DE RENNES, 83

BIBLIOTHÈQUE NATIONALE — R. F. — IMPRIMÉS

AVANT-PROPOS

Tous les morceaux contenus dans ce nouveau recueil sont extraits des ouvrages indiqués par les programmes officiels pour les classes moyennes. Plusieurs de ces morceaux ont une étendue assez considérable, surtout le dernier, qui offre une histoire complète. L'élève pourra donc se familiariser avec ses modèles, et comme les textes sont choisis parmi les plus intéressants, il y fera avec plaisir l'essai de ses forces. Sous la direction du maître, qui multipliera de vive voix ses remarques grammaticales, il s'enrichira d'une ample provision de mots et de tournures, et, après avoir traduit soigneusement tout l'ouvrage, il abordera sans peine les auteurs prescrits pour l'examen du baccalauréat.

COURS GRADUÉ DE VERSIONS ANGLAISES

Robinson Crusoé aperçoit sur le sable l'empreinte d'un pied d'homme.

It happened one day, about noon, going towards my boat, I was exceedingly surprised with the print of a man's foot on the shore, which was very plain to be seen in the sand. I stood like one thunderstruck, or as if I had seen an apparition; I listened, I looked round me, but I could hear nothing, nor see anything; I went up to a rising ground to look farther; I went up the shore and down the shore, but it was all one, I could see no other impression but that one. I went to it again to see if there were any more, and to observe if it might not be my fancy; but there was no room for that, for there was exactly the very print of a foot, toes, heel, and every part of a foot; how it came thither I knew not, nor could in the least imagine. But after innumerable fluttering thoughts, like a man perfectly confused and out of myself, I came home to my fortification, not feeling, as we say, the ground I went on, but terrified to the last degree, looking behind me at every two or three steps, mistaking every bush and tree, and fancying

every stump at a distance to be a man; nor it
is possible to describe how many various shapes my affrighted imagination represented
things to me in, how many wild ideas were
found every moment in my fancy, and what
strange unaccountable whimsies came into my
thoughts by the way.

DE FOE (1663-1731), *Robinson Crusoé.*

Robinson Crusoé sauve la vie de Vendredi.

1. — There was between the savages and my
castle the creek, which I mentioned often at
the first part of my story, when I landed my
cargoes out of the ship; and this I saw plainly
he must necessarily swim over, or the poor
wretch would be taken there : but when the savage escaping came thither, he made nothing of
it, though the tide was then up; but plunging
in, swam through in about thirty strokes, or
thereabouts, landed, and ran on with exceeding
strength and swiftness. When the three pursuers came to the creek, I found that two of
them could swim, but the third could not, and
that, standing on the other side, he looked at
the others, but went no farther, and soon
after went softly back again; which, as it
happened, was very well for him in the main.
I observed that the two who swam were yet
twice as long swimming over the creek as the
fellow was that fled from them. It came now
very warmly upon my thoughts, and indeed

irresistibly, that now was my time to get me a
servant, and perhaps a companion or assistant;
and that I was called plainly by Providence to
save this poor creature's life. I immediately got
down the ladders with all possible expedition,
fetched my two guns, for they were both but
at the foot of the ladders, as I observed above,
and getting up again with the same haste to
the top of the hill, clapped myself in the way
between the pursuers and the pursued, hallooing aloud to him that fled, who looking
back, was at first, perhaps, as much frighted
at me as they; but I beckoned with my hand to
him to come back; and in the mean time, I
slowly advanced towards the two that followed;
then rushing at once upon the foremost, I
knocked him down with the stock of my piece.

2. — I was loath to fire, because I would not
have the rest hear; though at that distance it
would not have been easily heard, and being
out of sight of the smoke too, they would not
have easily known what to make of it. Having
knocked this fellow down, the other who pursued with him stopped, as if he had been frighted, and I advanced apace towards him ; but
as I came nearer, I perceived presently he had
a bow and arrow, and was fitting it to shoot at
me ; so I was then necessitated to shoot at him
first, which I did, and killed him at the first
shot. The poor savage who fled, but had stopped,
though he saw both his enemies fallen and
killed, as he thought, yet was so frighted with
the fire and noise of my piece, that he stood

fellow with a red beard at the gate, who called himself the goodman of Ballengiech, who said he was come to dine with the king of Kippen. As soon as Buchanan heard these words, he knew that the king was come in person, and hastened down to kneel at James's feet, and to ask forgiveness for his insolent behaviour. But the king, who only meant to give him a fright, forgave him freely, and, going into the castle, feasted on his own venison which Buchanan had intercepted. Buchanan of Arnpryor. was afterwards called the king of Kippen.

(Contes d'un grand-père.)

Exécution de Marie Stuart.

1. — On the 8th February 1587, the Queen, still maintaining the same calm and undisturbed appearance which she had displayed at her pretended trial, was brought down to the great hall of the castle, where a scaffold was erected, on which were placed a block and a chair, the whole being covered with black cloth. The master of her household, sir Andrew Melville, was permitted to take a last leave of the mistress whom he had served long and faithfully. He burst into loud lamentations, bewailing her fate, and deploring his own in being destined to carry such news to Scotland. « Weep not, my good Melville, » said the Queen, « but rather rejoice; for thou shalt this day see Mary Stewart relieved from all her sorrows. » She

obtained permission, with some difficulty, that her maids should be allowed to attend her on the scaffold. It was objected to, that the extravagance of their grief might disturb the proceedings; she engaged for them that they would be silent.

2. — When the Queen was seated in the fatal chair, she heard the death warrant read by Beale, the clerk to the Privy Council, with an appearance of indifference; nor did she seem more attentive to the devotional exercises of the Dean of Peterborough, in which, as a Catholic, she could not conscientiously join. She implored the mercy of Heaven, after the form prescribed by her own Church. She then prepared herself for execution, taking off such parts of her dress as might interfere with the deadly blow. She quietly chid her maids, who were unable to withhold their cries of lamentation, and reminded them that she had engaged for their silence. Last of all, Mary laid her head on the block, which the executioner severed from her body with two strokes of his axe. The headsman held it up in his hand, and the Dean of Peterborough cried out, « So perish all Queen Elizabeth's enemies ! » No voice, save that of the Earl of Kent, could answer *Amen :* the rest were choked with sobs and tears.

Thus died Queen Mary, aged a little above forty-four years.

(Contes d'un grand-père.)

Naissance et éducation de Christophe Colomb.

1. — Christopher Columbus, or Colombo, as the name is written in Italian, was born in the city of Genoa, about the year 1435, of poor but reputable and meritorious parentage.

While very young, Columbus was taught reading, writing, grammar and arithmetic, and made some proficiency in drawing. He soon evinced a strong passion for geographical knowledge, and an irresistible inclination for the sea; and in after life, when he looked back upon his career with a solemn and superstitious feeling, he regarded this early determination of his mind as an impulse from the deity guiding him to the studies, and inspiring him with the inclinations, proper to fit him for the high decrees he was destined to accomplish. His father, seing the bent of his mind, endeavoured to give him an education suitable for maritime life. He sent him, therefore, to the University of Pavia, where he was instructed in geometry, geography, astronomy, and navigation; he acquired also a familiar knowledge of the Latin tongue, which at that time was the medium of instruction, and the language of the schools.

2. — He remained but a short time at Pavia, barely sufficient to give him the rudiments of the necessary sciences; the thorough acquaintance with them which he displayed in after life must have been the result of diligent self-schooling, and of casual hours of study, amidst the cares

and vicissitudes of a rugged and wandering
life. He was one of those men of strong natural
genius, who appear to form themselves; who,
from having to contend at their very outset
with privations and impediments, acquire an
intrepidity in braving, and a facility in van-
quishing difficulties. Such men learn to effect
great purposes with small means, supplying the
deficiency of the latter by the resources of their
own energy and invention. This is one of the
remarkable features in the history of Columbus.
In every undertaking, the scantiness and appa-
rent insufficiency of his means enhance the
grandeur of his achievements.

Son premier voyage. — Découverte de l'île de San-Salvador.

1. — It was early in the morning of Friday the
3rd of August, 1492, that Columbus set sail from
the bar of Saltes, a small island formed by the
rivers Odiel and Tinto, in front of Palos, stee-
ring for the Canary Islands, from whence he
intended to strike due West.

On the third day after setting sail, the Pinta
made signal of distress, her rudder being broken and unhung. This was suspected to have
been done through the contrivance of the ow-
ners, Gomez Rascon and Christoval Quintero,
to disable the vessel, and cause her to be left
behind. Columbus was much disturbed at this
occurence. It gave him a foretaste of the diffi-

culties to be apprehended, from people partly enlisted on compulsion, and full of doubt and foreboding.

Martin Alonso Pinzon, who commanded the Pinta, secured the rudder with cords, but these fastenings soon gave way, and the caravel proving defective in other respects, Columbus remained three weeks cruising among the Canary Islands, in search of another vessel to replace her. Not being able to find one, the Pinta was repaired, and furnished with a new rudder. The lateen sails of the Niña were also altered into square sails, that she might work more steadily and securely.

2. — While making these repairs and taking in wood and water, Columbus was informed that three Portuguese caravels had been seen hovering off the Island of Ferro. Dreading some hostile stratagem, on the part of the king of Portugal, in revenge for his having embarked in the service of Spain, he put to sea early in the morning of the 6th of September, but for three days a profound calm detained the vessels within a short distance of the land. This was a tantalizing delay, for Columbus trembled lest something should occur to defeat his expedition, and was impatient to find himself far upon the ocean, out of sight of either land or sail; which, in the pure atmospheres of these latitudes, may be descried at an immense distance.

On Sunday, the 9th of September, as day broke, he beheld Ferro about nine leagues distant; he was in the very neighbourhood, therefore, where the Portuguese caravels had been seen. Fortunately a breeze sprang up with the sun, and in the course of the day, the heights of Ferro gradually faded from the horizon.

3. — On losing sight of this last trace of land, the hearts of the crews failed them, for they seemed to have taken leave of the world. Behind them was every thing dear to the heart of man — country, family, friends, life itself; before them every thing was chaos, mystery, and peril. In the perturbation of the moment, they despaired of ever more seeing their homes. Many of the rugged seamen shed tears, and some broke into loud lamentations. Columbus tried in every way to soothe their distress, describing the splendid countries to which he expected to conduct them, and promising them land, riches, and every thing that could arouse their cupidity or inflame their imaginations; nor were these promises made for purposes of deception, for he certainly believed he should realize them all.

He now gave orders to the commanders of the other vessels, in case they should be separated by any accident, to continue directly westward; but that, after sailing seven hundred leagues, they should lay by from midnight until daylight, as at about that distance he confidently expected to find land.

When about one hundred and fifty leagues west of Ferro, they fell in with a part of a mast of a large vessel, and the crews, tremblingly alive to every portent, looked with a rueful eye upon this fragment of a wreck, drifting ominously at the entrance of these unknown seas.

4. — On the 13th of September, in the evening, Columbus, for the first time, noticed the variation of the needle, a phenomenon which had never before been remarked. He at first made no mention of it, lest his people should be alarmed : but it soon attracted the attention of the pilots, and filled them with consternation. It seemed as if the very laws of nature were changing as they advanced, and that they were entering another world, subject to unknown influences. They apprehended that the compass was about to lose its mysterious virtues, and, without this guide, what was to become of them in a vast and trackless ocean ? Columbus tasked his science and ingenuity for reasons with which to allay their terrors. He told them that the direction of the needle was not to the polar star, but to some fixed and invisible point. The variation, therefore, was not caused by any fallacy in the compass, but by the movement of the north star itself, which, like the other heavenly bodies, had its changes and revolutions, and every day described a circle round the pole. The high opinion they entertained of Columbus as a profound astronomer gave weight to his theory, and their alarm subsided.

5. — They now began to see large patches of herbs and weeds all drifting from the west.

Some were such as grow abou t rocksor in rivers, and as green as if recently washed from the land. On one of the patches was a live crab. They saw also a white tropical bird, of a kind which never sleeps upon the sea ; and tunny fish played about the ships. Columbus now supposed himself arrived in the weedy sea described by Aristotle, into which certain ships of Cadiz had been driven by an impetuous east wind.

As he advanced, there were various other signs that gave great animation to the crews ; many birds were seen flying from the west ; there was a cloudiness in the north, such as often hangs over land; and at sunset the imagination of the seamen, aided by their desires, would shape those clouds into distant islands. Every one was eager to be the first to behold and announce the wished for shore; for the sovereigns had promised a pension of thirty crowns to whomsoever should first discover land. Columbus sounded occasionally with a line of two hundred fathoms, but found no bottom.

6. — For three days there was a continuance of light summer airs, from the southward and westward, and the sea was as smooth as a mirror. The crews now became uneasy at the calmness of the weather. They observed that the contrary winds they experienced were transient and unsteady, and so light as not to ruffle the surface of the sea ; the only winds of constancy and force were from the east, and even those had not power to disturb the torpid still-

ness of the ocean : there was a risk, therefore, either of perishing amidst stagnant and shoreless waters, or of being prevented, by contrary winds, from ever returning to their native country.

Columbus continued, with admirable patience, to reason with these absurd fancies, but in vain ; when fortunately there came on a heavy swell of the sea, unaccompanied by wind, a phenomenon that often occurs in the broad ocean, caused by the impulse of some past gale, or distant current of wind. It was, nevertheless, regarded with astonishment by the mariners, and dispelled the imaginary terrors occasioned by the calm.

7. — The situation of Columbus was daily becoming more and more critical. The impatience of the seamen rose to absolute mutiny. They gathered together in the retired parts of the ships, at first in little knots of two and three, which gradually increased and became formidable, joining in murmurs and menaces against the admiral. They exclaimed against him as an ambitious desperado, who, in a mad phantasy, had determined to do something extravagant, to render himself notorious. What obligation bound them to persist, or when were the terms of their agreement to be considered as fulfilled? They had already penetrated into seas untraversed by a sail, and where man had never before adventured. Were they to sail on until they should perish, or until all return with their frail ships should become im-

possible ? Who would blame them, should they consult their safety and return ? The admiral was a foreigner, without friends or influence. His scheme had been condemned by the learned as idle and visionary, and discountenanced by people of all ranks. There was, therefore, no party on his side, but rather a large number who would be gratified by his failure.

Such are some of the reasonings by which these men prepared themselves for open rebellion. Some even proposed, as an effectual mode of silencing all after-complaints of the admiral, that they should throw him into the sea, and give out that he had fallen overboard, while contemplating the stars and signs of the heavens, with his astronomical instruments.

8. — Columbus was not ignorant of these secret cabals, but he kept a serene and steady countenance, soothing some with gentle words, stimulating the pride or the avarice of others, ad openly menacing the most refactory with punishment. New hopes diverted them for a time. On the 25th of September, Martin Alonso Pinzon mounted on the stern of his vessel, and shouted : « Land ! land ! Señor, I claim the reward ! » There was, indeed, such an appearance of land in the south-west, that Columbus threw himself upon his knees, and returned thanks to God, and all the crews joined in chanting *Gloria in excelsis*. The ships altered their course, and stood all night to the southwest ; but the morning light put an end to all

their hopes as to a dream: the fancied land pro-
ved to be nothing but an evening cloud, and
had vanished in the night.

For several days they continued on with al-
ternate hopes and murmurs, until the various
signs of land became so numerous that the seamen, from a state of despondency, passed to
one of high excitement. Eager to obtain the
promised pension, they were continually giving
the cry of land ; until Columbus declared that
should any one give a notice of the kind, and
land not be discovered within three days afterwards, he should thenceforth forfeit all claim
to the reward.

9. — On the 7th of October, they had come
seven hundred and fifty leagues, the distance
at which Columbus had computed to find the
Island of Cipango. There were great flights of
small field-birds to the south-west, which semeed
to indicate some neighbouring land in that direction, where they were sure of food and a resting-
place. Yielding to the solicitations of Martin Alonso Pinzon, and his brothers, Columbus, on the
evening of the 7th, altered his course, therefore,
to the west-south-west. As he advanced, the
signs of land increased ; the birds came singing
about the ships, and herbage floated by as fresh
and green as if recently from shore. When,
however, on the evening of the third day of
this new course, the seamen beheld the sun go
down upon a shoreless horizon, they again
broke forth into loud clamours, and insisted
upon abandoning the voyage. Columbus endea-

voured to pacify them by gentle words and liberal promises; but finding these only increased their violence, he assumed a different tone, and told them it was useless to murmur; the expedition had been sent by the sovereigns to seek the Indies, and happen what might, he was determined to persevere, until, by the blessing of God, he should accomplish the enterprise.

He was now at open defiance with his crew, and his situation would have been desperate, but, fortunately, the manifestations of land on the following day were such as no longer to admit of doubt. A green fish, such as keeps about rocks, swam by the ships; and a branch of thorn, with berries on it, floated by; they picked up, also, a reed, a small board, and above all, a staff artificially carved. All gloom and murmuring was now at an end, and throughout the day each one was on the watch for the long-sought land.

10. — In the evening, when, according to custom, the mariners had sung the *Salve Regina*, or vesper hymn to the Virgin, Columbus made an impressive address to his crew, pointing out the goodness of God in thus conducting them by soft and favouring breezes across a tranquil ocean to the promised land. He expressed a strong confidence of making land that very night, and ordered that a vigilant lookout should be kept from the forecastle, promising to whomsoever should make the discovery a doublet of velvet, in addition to the pension to be given by the sovereigns.

The breeze had been fresh all day, with more sea than usual ; at sunset they stood again to the west, and were ploughing the waves at a rapid rate, the Pinta keeping the lead from her superior sailing. The greatest animation prevailed throughout the ships; not an eye was closed that night. As the evening darkened, Columbus took his station on the top of the castle or cabin on the high poop of his vessel. However he might carry a cheerful and confident countenance, during the day, it was to him a time of the most painful anxiety, and now, when he was wrapped from observation by the shades of night, he maintained an intense and unremitting watch, ranging his eye along the dusky horizon, in search of the most vague indications of land. Suddenly, about ten o'clock, he thought he beheld a light glimmering at a distance. Fearing that his eager hopes might deceive him, he called to Pedro Gutierrez, gentleman of the king's bedchamber, and demanded whether he saw a light in that direction ; the latter replied in the affirmative.

11. — They continued on their course until two in the morning, when a gun from the Pinta gave the joyful signal of land. It was first discovered by a mariner named Rodriguez Bermejo, resident of Triana. The land was now clearly seen about two leagues distant, where upon they took in sail, and laid to, waiting impatiently for the dawn.

The thoughts and feelings of Columbus in this little space of time must have been tumul-

tuous and intense. At length, in spite of every
difficulty and danger, he had accomplished his
ob ect.The great mystery of the ocean was
revealed; his theory, which had been the scoff
of sages, was triumphantly established; he had
secured to himself a glory which must be as
durable as the world itself.

When the day dawned, Columbus saw before
him a level and beautiful island, several leagues in extent, of great freshness and verdure,
and covered with trees like a continual or-
chard.

As they approached the shores, they were
delighted by the beauty and grandeur of the
forests; the variety of unknown fruits on the
trees which overhung the shores; the purity
and suavity of the athmosphere, and the crystal
transparency of the seas which bathe these islands. On landing, Columbus threw himself
upon his knees, kissed the earth, and returned
thanks to God with tears of joy. His example
was followed by his companions, whose breasts,
indeed, were full to overflowing. Columbus
then rising, drew his sword, displayed the royal
standard, and took possession in the names of
the Castilian sovereigns, giving the island the
name of San Salvador.

Washington Irving (1783-1859), Vie et
Voyages de Christophe Colomb.

Histoire de Rip Van Winkle.

1.— WHOEVER has made a voyage up the Hudson must remember the Kaatskill mountains. They are a dismembered branch of the great Appalachian family, and are seen away to the west of the river, swelling up to a noble height, and lording it over the surrounding country. Every change of season, every change of weather, indeed, every hour of the day, produces some change in the magical hues and shapes of these mountains, and they are regarded by all the good wives, far and near, as perfect barometers. When the weather is fair and settled, they are clothed in blue and purple, and print their bold outlines on the clear evening sky; but sometimes, when the rest of the landscape is cloudless, they will gather a hood of gray vapour about their summits, which, in the last rays of the setting sun, will glow and light up like a crown of glory.

At the foot of these fairy mountains, the voyager may have descried the light smoke curling up from a village, whose shingle-roofs gleam among the trees just where the blue tints of the upland melt away into the fresh green of the nearer landscape. It is a little village, of great antiquity, having been founded by some of the Dutch colonists in the early times of the province, just about the beginning of the government of the good Peter Stuyvesant (may he rest in peace!) and there were some of the houses of the original settlers standing within a few years, built of small yellow bricks brought from Holland, having latticed windows and gable fronts, surmounted with weathercocks.

2. — In that same village, and in one of these very houses (which, to tell the precise truth, was sadly time-worn and weather-beaten), there lived many years since, while the country was yet a province of Great Britain, a simple good-natured fellow, of the name of Rip Van Winkle. He was a descendant of the Van Winkles who figured so gallantly in the chivalrous days of Peter Stuyvesant, and accompanied him to the siege of Fort Christina. He inherited, however, but little of the martial character of his ancestors. I have observed that he was a simple good-natured man : he was, moreover, a kind neighbour, and an obedient hen-pecked husband. Indeed, to the latter circumstance might be owing that meekness of spirit which gained him such universal popularity; for those men are most apt to be obsequious and conciliating abroad, who are under the discipline of shrews at home. The children of the village, too, would shout with joy whenever he approached. He assisted at their sports, made their playthings, taught them to fly kites and shoot marbles, and told them long stories of ghosts, witches, and Indians. Whenever he went dodging about the village, he was surrounded by a troop of them, hanging on his skrits, clambering on his back, and playing a thousand tricks on him with impunity; and not a dog would bark at him throughout the neighbourhood.

3.—The great error in Rip's composition was an insuperable aversion to all kinds of profitable labour. It could not be from the want of assiduity or perseverance; for he would sit on a wet rock, with a rod as long and heavy as a Tartar's lance, and fish all day without a murmur, even though he should not be encouraged by a single nibble. He would carry a fowling-piece on his shoulder for hours together, trudging through woods and swamps, and up hill and down dale, to shoot a few squirrels or wild pigeons. He would never refuse to assist a neighbour even in the roughest toil, and was a foremost man at all country frolics for husking Indian corn, or building stone fences ; the women of the village, too, used to employ him to run their errands, and to do such little odd jobs as their less obliging husbands would not do for them. In a word, Rip was ready to attend to anybody's business but his own, but as to doing family duty, and keeping his farm in order, he found it impossible.

In fact, he declared it was of no use to work on his farm; it was the most pestilent little piece of ground in the whole country; everything about it went wrong, and would go wrong, in spite of him. His fences were continually falling to pieces; his cow would either go astray, or get among the cabbages : weeds were sure to grow quicker in his fields than anywhere else ; the rain always made a point of setting in just as he had some out-door work to do ; so that though his patrimonial

estate had dwindled away under his manage-
ment, acre by acre, until there was little more
left than a mere patch of Indian corn and po-
tatoes, yet it was the worst conditioned farm
in the neighbourhood.

4. — His children, too, were as ragged and
wild as if they belonged to nobody. His son
Rip, an urchin begotten in his own likeness,
promised to inherit the habits, with the old
clothes of his father. He was generally seen
trooping like a colt at his mother's heels,
equipped in a pair of his father's cast-off galli-
gaskins, which he had much ado to hold up
with one hand, as a fine lady does her train in
bad weather.

Rip Van Winkle, however, was one of those
happy mortals, of foolish, well-oiled disposi-
tions, who take the world easy, eat white bread
or brown, whichever can be got with least
thought or trouble, and would rather starve on
a penny than work for a pound. If left to him·
self, he would have whistled life away in perfect contentment ; but his wife kept continually
dinning in his ears about his idleness, his
carelessness, and the ruin he was bringing on
his family. Morning, noon, and night, her
tongue was incessantly going, and everything
he said or did was sure to produce a torrent
of household eloquence. Rip had but one way
of replying to all lectures of the kind, and that,
by frequent use, had grown into a habit. He
shrugged his shoulders, shook his head, cast
up his eyes, but said nothing. This, however,

always provoked a fresh volley from his wife; so that he was fain to draw off his forces, and take to the outside of the house, the only side which, in thruth, belongs to a hen-pecked husband.

5.—Rip's sole domestic adherent was his dog Wolf, who was as much hen-pecked as his master; for Dame Van Winkle regarded them as companions in idleness, and even looked upon Wolf with an evil eye, as the cause of his master's going so often astray. True it is, in all points of spirit befitting an honourable dog, he was as courageous an animal as ever scoured the woods — but what courage can withstand the ever-during and all besetting terrors of a woman's tongue? The moment Wolf entered the house, his crest fell, his tail drooped to the ground, or curled betwen his legs, he sneaked about with a gallows air, casting many a side-long glance at Dame Van Winkle, and at the least flourish of a broom stick or ladle, he would fly to the door with yelping precipitation.

Times grew worse and worse with Rip Van Winkle as years of matrimony rolled on; a tart temper never mellows with age, and a sharp tongue is the only edged tool that grows keener with constant use. For a long while he used to console himself, when driven from home, by frequenting a kind of perpetual club of the sages, philosophers, and other idle personages of the village; which held its sessions on a bench before a small inn, designated by a rubicund portrait of his Majesty George the Third. Here they used to sit in the shade. through a long lazy summer's day, talking listlessly over village gossip, or telling endless sleepy stories about nothing. But it would have been worth any statesman's money to have heard the profound discussions that sometimes took place, when by chance an old newspaper fell into their hands from some passing travel- ler. How solemnly they would listen to the contents, as drawled out by Derrick Van Bummel, the schoolmaster, a dapper learned little man, who was not to be daunted by the most gigantic word in the dictionary : and how sagely they would deliberate upon public events some months after they had taken place.

6. — The opinions of this junto were comple- tely controlled by Nicholas Vedder, a patriarch of the village, and landlord of the inn, at the door of which he took his seat from morning till night, just moving sufficiently to avoid the sun and keep in the shade of a large tree ; so that the neighbours could tell the hour by his movements as accurately as by a sundial. It is true he was rarely heard to speak, but smoked his pipe incessantly. His adherents, however (for every great man has his adherents), perfectly understood him, and knew how to gather his opinions. When anything that was read or related displeased him, he was observed to smoke his pipe vehemently, and to send forth short, frequent, and angry puffs,

but when pleased he would inhale the smoke slowly and tranquilly, and emit it in light and placid clouds ; and sometimes, taking the pipe from his mouth, and letting the fragrant vapour curl about his nose, would gravely nod his head in token of perfect approbation.

From even this stronghold the unlucky Rip was at length routed by his termagant wife, who would suddenly break in upon the tranquillity of the assemblage and call the members all to naught ; nor was that august personage, Nicholas Vedder himself, sacred from the daring tongue of this terrible virago, who charged him outright with encouraging her husband in habits of idleness.

7. — Poor Rip was at last reduced almost to despair ; and his only alternative, to escape from the labour of the farm and clamour of his wife, was to take gun in hand and stroll away into the woods. Here he would sometimes seat himself at the foot of a tree, and share the contents of his wallet with Wolf, with whom he sympathised as a fellow-sufferer in persecution. " Poor Wolf " he would say, " thy mistress leads thee a dog's life of it; but never mind, my lad, whilst I live thou shalt never want a friend to stand by thee! " Wolf would wag his tail, look wistfully in his master's face, and if dogs can feel pity, I verily believe he reciprocated the sentiment with all his heart.

In a long ramble of the kind on a fide autumnal day, Rip had unconsciously scrambled to one of the highest parts of the Kaatskill mountains.

He was after his favourite sport of squirrel-shooting, and the still solitudes had echoed and reechoed with the reports of his gun. Panting and fatigued, he threw himself, late in the afternoon, on a green knoll, covered with mountain herbage, that crowned the brow of a precipice. From an opening between the trees he could overlook all the lower country for many a mile of rich woodland. He saw at a distance the lordly Hudson, far, far below him, moving on its silent but majestic course, with the reflection of a purple cloud, or the sail of a lagging bark, here and there sleeping on its glassy bosom, and at last losing itself in the blue highlands.

8. — On the other side he looked down into a deep mountain glen, wild, lonely, and shagged, the bottom filled with fragments from the impending cliffs, and scarcely lighted by the reflected rays of the setting sun. For some time Rip lay musing on this scene; evening was gradually advancing; the mountains began to throw their long blue shadows over the valleys; he saw that it would be dark long before he could reach the village, and he heaved a heavy sigh when he thought of encountering the terrors of Dame Van Winkle.

As he was about to descend, he heard a voice from a distance, hallooing, ‘‘ Rip Van Winkle! Rip Wan Winkle ! ’’ He looked round, but could see nothing but a crow winging its solitary flight across the mountain. He thought his fancy must have deceived him, and turned again to descend, when he heard the same cry ring through the still evening air, " Rip Van Winkle! Rip Van Winkle! " — at the same time Wolf bristled up his back, and, giving a loud growl, skulked to his master's side, looking fearfully down into the glen. Rip now felt a vague apprehension stealing over him ; he looked anxiously in the same direction, and perceived a strange figure slowly toiling up the rocks, and bending under the weight of something he carried on his back. He was surprised to see any human being in this lonely and unfrequented place ; but supposing it to be some one of the neighbourhood in need of his assistance, he hastened down to yield it.

9.—On nearer approach he was still more surprised at the singularity of the stranger's appearance. He was a short, square-built, old fellow, with thick bushy hair and a grizzled beard. His dress was of the antique Dutch fashion — a cloth jerkin, strapped round the waist — several pairs of breeches, the outer one of ample volume, decorated with rows of buttons down the sides, and bunches at the knees. He bore on his shoulder a stout keg, that seemed full of liquor, and made signs for Rip to approach and assist him with the load. Though rather shy and distrustful of this new acquaintance, Rip complied with his usual alacrity ; and mutually relieving each other, they clambered up a narrow gully, apparently the dry bed of a mountain torrent. As they ascended, Rip every now and then heard long rolling peals, like distant thunder, that seemed to issue out of a deep ravine, or rather cleft, between lofty rocks, toward which their rugged path conducted. He paused for an instant, but supposing it to be the muttering of one of those transient thunder-showers which often take place in mountain heights, he proceeded. Passing through the ravine, they came to a hollow, like a small amphitheatre, surrounded by perpendicular precipices, over the brinks of which impending trees shot their branches, so that you only caught glimpses of the azure sky and the bright evening cloud. During the whole time, Rip and his companion had laboured on in silence, for though the former marvelled greatly what could be the object of carrying a keg of liquor up this wild mountain; yet there was something strange and incomprehensible about the unknown, that inspired awe and checked familiarity.

10. — On entering the amphitheatre, new objects of wonder presented themselves. On a level spot in the centre was a company of odd-looking personages playing at nine-pins. They were dressed in a quaint outlandish fashion ; some wore short doublets, others jerkins, with long knives in their belts, and most of them had enormous breeches, of similar style with that of the guide's. Their visages, too, were peculiar; one had a large head, broad face, and small piggish eyes; the face of another seemed to consist entirely of nose, and was surmounted

by a white sugar-loaf hat, set off with a little red cock's tail. They all had beards, of various shapes and colours. There was one who seemed to be the commander. He was a stout old gentleman, with a weather-beaten countenance; he wore a laced doublet, broad belt and hanger, high-crowned hat and feather, red stockings, and high-heeled shoes, with roses in them. The whole group reminded Rip of the figures in an old Flemish painting, in the parlour of Dominie Van Shaick, the village parson, and which had been brought over from Holland at the time of the settlement.

What seemed particularly odd to Rip was, that though these folks were evidently amusing themselves, yet they maintained the gravest faces, the most mysterious silence, and were, withal, the most melancholy party of pleasure he had ever witnessed. Nothing interrupted the stillness of the scene but the noise of the balls, which, whenever they were rolled, echoed along the mountains like rumbling peals of thunder.

11. — As Rip and his companion approached them, they suddenly desisted from their play, and stared at him with such fixed, statue-like gaze, and such strange, uncouth, lack-lustre countenances, that his heart turned within him and his knees smote together. His companion now emptied the contents of the keg into large flagons, and made signs to him to wait upon the company. He obeyed with fear and trembling ; they quaffed the liquor in profound

silence, and then returned to their game.

By degrees Rip's awe and apprehension sub-sided. He even ventured, when no eye was fixed upon him, to taste the beverage,. which he found had much of the flavour of excellent Hollands. He was naturally a thirsty soul, and was soon tempted to repeat the draught. One taste provoked another; and he reiterated his visits to the flagon so often, that at length his senses were overpowered, his eyes swam in his head, his head gradually declined, and he fell into a deep sleep.

On waking, he found himself on the green knoll whence he had first seen the old man of the glen. He rubbed his eyes — it was a bright sunny morning. The birds were hopping and twittering among the bushes, and the eagle was wheeling aloft, and breasting the pure mountain breeze. " Surely, " thought Rip, " I have not slept here all night. " He recalled the occurrences before he fell asleep. The strange man whit the keg of liquor — the mountain ravine — the wild retreat among the rocks — the wo-begone party at nine-pins — the flagon — " Oh! that flagon! that wicked flagon! " thought Rip ; " what excuse shall I make to Dame Van Winkle ? "

12. — He looked round for his gun, but in place of the clean well-oiled fowling-piece, he found an old firelock lying by him, the barrel incrus-ted with rust, the lock falling off, and the stock worm-eaten. He now suspected that the grave roisters of the mountain had put a trick upon

him, and having dosed him with liquor, had robbed him of his gun. Wolf, too, had disappeared, but he might have strayed away after a squirrel or partridge. He whistled after him and shouted his name, but all in vain; the echoes repeated his whistle and shout, but no dog was to be seen.

He determined to revisit the scene of the last evening's gambol, and, if he met with any of the party, to demand his dog and gun. As he rose to walk, he found himself stiff in the joints, and wanting in his usual activity. "These moutain beds do not agree with me," thought Rip; " and if this frolic should lay me up with a fit of rheumatism, I shall have a blessed time with Dame Van Winkle." With some difficulty he got down into the glen : he found the gully up which he and his companion had ascended the preceding evening; but, to his astonishment, a mountain stream was now foaming down it — leaping from rock to rock, and filling the glen with babbling murmurs. He, however, made shift to scramble up its sides, working his toilsome way through thickets of birch, sassafras, and witch-hazel, and sometimes tripped up or entangled by the wild grape-vines that twisted their coils or tendrils from tree to tree, and spread a kind of network in his path.

13.— At length he reached to where the ravine had opened through the cliffs to the amphitheatre ; but no traces of such opening remained. The rocks presented a high impenetrable wall,

over which the torrent came tumbling in a sheet
of feathery foam, and fell into a broad deep
basin, black from the shadows of the surrounding forest. Here, then, poor Rip was brought to
a stand. He again called and whistled after his
dog; he was only answered by the cawing of a
flock of idle crows sporting high in air about a
dry tree that overhung a sunny precipice; and
who, secure in their elevation, seemed to look
down and scoff at the poor man's perplexities.
What was to be done ? — the morning was
passing away, and Rip felt famished for want
of his breakfast. He grieved to give up his dog
and his gun; he dreaded to meet his wife; but
it would not do to starve among the moutains.
He shook his head, shouldered the rusty firelock, and with a heart full of trouble and anxiety, turned his steps homeward.

As he approached the village, he met a number of people, but none whom he knew, which
somewhat surprised him, for he had thought
himself acquainted with every one in the country round. Their dress, too, was of a different
fashion from that to which he was accustomed.
They all stared at him with equal marks of
surprise, and, whenever they cast their eyes
upon him, invariably stroked their chins. The
constant recurrence of this gesture induced Rip,
involuntarily, to do the same — when, to his
astonishment, he found his beard had grown
a foot long !

14. — He had now entered the skirts of the
village. A troop of strange children ran at his

heels, hooting after him, and pointing at his grey beard. The dogs, too, not one of which he recognised for an old acquaintance, barked at him as he passed; the very village was altered; it was larger and more populous. There were rows of houses which he had never seen before, and those which had been his familiar haunts had disappeared. Strange names were over the doors — strange faces at the windows — everything was strange. — His mind now misgave him : he began to doubt whether both he and the world around him were not bewitched. Surely this was his native village, which he had left but the day before. There stood the Kaatskill mountains — there ran the silver Hudson at a distance — there was every hill and dale precisely as it had always been. Rip was sorely perplexed. " That flagon last night " thought he, " has addled my poor head sadly ! "

It was with some difficulty that he found the way to his own house, which he approached with silent awe, expecting every moment to hear the shrill voice of Dame Van Winkle. He found the house gone to decay — tho roof fallen in, the windows shattered, and the doors off the hinges. A half-starved dog, that looked like Wolf, was skulking about it. Rip called him by name, but the cur snarled, showed his teeth, and passed on. This was an unkind cut indeed — " My very dog, " sighed poor Rip, " has forgotten me ! "

15. —He entered the house, which, to tell the

truth, Dame Van Winkle had always kept in neat order. It was empty, forlorn, and apparently abandoned. The desolateness overcame all his connubial fears — he called loudly for his wife and children — the lonely chambers rang for a moment with his voice, and then all again was silence.

He now hurried forth, and hastened to his old resort, the village inn — but it too was gone. A large rickety wooden building stood in its place, with great gaping windows, some of them broken and mended with old hats and petticoats, and over the door was painted, " The Union Hotel, by Jonathan Doolittle ". Instead of the great tree that used to shelter the quiet little Dutch inn of yore, there was now reared a tall naked pole, with something on the top that looked like a red nightcap; and from it was fluttering a flag, on which was a singular assemblage of stars and stripes — all this was strange and incomprehensible. He recognised on the sign, however, the ruby face of King George, under which he had smoked so many a peaceful pipe ; but even this was singularly metamorphosed. The red coat was changed for one of blue and buff, a sword was held in the hand instead of a sceptre, the head was decorated with a cocked hat, and underneath was painted in large characters, GENERAL WASHINGTON.

16. — There was, as usual, a crowd of folks about the door, but none that Rip recollected. The very character of the people seemed chan-

ged. There was a busy, bustling, disputatious tone about it, instead of the accustomed phlegm and drowsy tranquillity. He looked in vain for the sage Nicholas Vedder, with his broad face, double chin, and fair long pipe, uttering clouds of tobacco smoke instead of idle speeches; or Van Bummel, the schoolmaster, doling forth the contents of an ancient newspaper. In place of these, a lean, bilious looking fellow, with his pockets full of hand-bills, was haranguing vehemently about rights of citizens — elections — members of congress — liberty — Bunker's Hill — heroes of seventy-six — and other words, which were a perfect Babylonish jargon to the bewildered Van Winkle.

The appearance of Rip, with his long grizzled beard, his rusty fowling-piece, his uncouth dress, and an army of women and children at his heels, soon attracted the attention of the tavern politicians. They crowded round him, eyeing him from head to foot, with great curiosity. The orator busted up to him, and, drawing him partly aside, inquired " on which side he voted"? Rip stared in vacant stupidity. Another short but busy little fellow pulled him by the arm, and rising on tiptoe, inquired in his ear, " Whether he was Federal or Democrat?" Rip was esqually at a loss, to comprehend the question ; when a knowing self-important old gentleman, in a sharp cocked hat, made his way through the crowd, putting them to the right and left with his elbows as he passed, and planting himself before Van Winkle, with one arm akimbo, the other resting on his cane, his keen eyes and sharp hat penetrating, as it were, into his very soul, demanded in an austere tone, "What brought him to the election with a gun on his shoulder, and a mob at his heels, and whether he meant to breed a riot in the village ?" — " Alas ! gentlemen," cried Rip, somewhat dismayed, " I am a poor quiet man, a native of the place, and a loyal subject of the king. God bless him ! "

17. —Here a general shout burst from the bystanders — " A tory ! a tory ! a spy ! a refugee ! hustle him ! away with him ! " It was with great difficulty that the self-important man in the cocked hat restored order ; and having assumed a tenfold austerity of brow, demanded again of the unknown culprit what he came there for, and whom he was seeking ? The poor man humbly assured him that he meant no harm, but merely came there in search of some of his neighbours, who used to keep about the tavern.

"Well — who are they? — name them. "

Rip bethought himself a moment, and inquired. "Where's Nicholas Wedder?"

There was a silence for a little while, when an old man replied in thin piping voice, "Nicholas Vedder ! why, he is dead and gone these eighteen years! There was a wooden tombstone in the churchyard that used to tell all about him, but that's rotten and gone too".

"Were's Brom Dutcher?"

"Oh, he went off to the army in the beginning of the war: some say he was killed at the storming of Stony Point — others say he was drowned in a squall at the foot of Antony's Nose . I don't know — he never came back again."

" Were's Van Bummel, the schoolmaster ?

" He went off to the wars too, was a great militia general, and is now in Congress."

Rip's heart died away at hearing of these sad changes in his home and friends, and finding himself thus alone in the world. Every answer puzzled him too, by treating of such enormous lapses of time, and of matters which he could not understand : war — congress — Stony Point; he had no courage to ask after any more friends, but cried out in despair, "Does nobody here know Rip Van Winkle ?"

" Oh, Rip Van Winkle !" exclaimed two or three, "Oh, to be sure ! that's Rip Van Winkle yonder, leaning against the tree."

18. —Rip looked, and beheld a precise counterpart of himself as he went up the mountain : apparently as lazy, and certainly as ragged. The poor fellow was now completely confounded. He doubted his own identity, and whether he was himself or another man. In the midst of his bewilderment, the man in the cocked hat demanded who he was, and what was his name?

" God knows," exclaimed he, at his wit's end; " I'm not myself — I'm somebody else —that's me yonder—no—that's somebody else got into my shoes — I was myself last night, but I fell asleep on the montain, and they've changed my gun, and everything's changed, and I am changed, and I can't tell what's my name, or who I am !''

The by-standers began now to look at each other, nod, wink significantly, and tap their fingers against their foreheads. There was a whisper, also, about securing the gun, and keeping the old fellow from doing mischief, at the very suggestion of which the self-important man in the cocked hat retired with some precipitation. At this critical moment a fresh comely woman pressed through the throng to get a peep at the grey-bearded man. She had a chubby child in her arms, which, frightened at his looks, began to cry. ''Hush, Rip,'' cried she, '' hush, you little fool, the old man won't hurt you.'' The name of the child, the air of the mother, the tone of her voice, all awakened a train of recollections in his mind.

'' What is your name, my good woman ?'' asked he.

'' Judith Gardenier.''

'' And your father's name ?''

'' Ah, poor man, Rip Van Winkle was his name, but it's twenty years since he went away from home with his gun, and never has been heard of since — his dog came home without him, but whether he shot himself, or was carried away by the Indians, nobody can tell. I was then but a little girl.''

19. — Rip had but one question more; but he put it with a faltering voice :

'' Where's your mother ?''

 " Oh, she too had died but a short time since ; she broke a blood-vessel in a fit of passion at a New England pedler.

There was a drop of comfort, at least, in this intelligence. The honest man could contain himself no longer. He caught his daughter and her child in his arms. " I am your father !" cried he — " Young Rip Van Winkle once — old Rip Van Winkle now ! — Does nobody know poor Rip Van Winkle ?"

All stood amazed until an old woman, tottering out from among the crowd, put her hand to her brow and peering under it in his face for a moment, exclaimed, " Sure enough ! it is Rip Van Winkle — it is himself ! Welcome home again, old neighbour. — Why, where have you been these twenty long years ?"

Rip's story was soon told, for the whole twenty years had been to him but as one night. The neighbours stared when they heard it ; some were seen to wink at each other, and put their tongues in their cheeks : and the self-important man in the cocked hat, who, when the alarm was over, had returned to the field, screwed down the corners of his mouth, and shook his head — upon which there was a general shaking of the head throughout the assemblage.

20. — It was determined, however, to take the opinion of old Peter Vanderdonk, who was seen slowly advancing up the road. He was a descendant of the historian of that name, who wrote one of the earliest accounts of the pro-

vince. Peter was the most ancient inhabitant of the village, and well versed in all the wonderful events and traditions of the neighbourhood. He recollected Rip at once, and corroborated his story in the most satisfactory manner. He assured the company that it was a fact, handed down from his ancestor the historian, that the Kaatskill mountains had always been haunted by strange beings. That it was affirmed that the great Hendrick Hudson, the first discoverer of the river and country, kept a kind of vigil there every twenty years with his crew of the Half-moon; being permitted in this way to revisit the scenes of his enterprise, and keep a guardian eye upon the river and the great city called by is name. That his father had once seen them in their old Dutch dresses playing at nine-pins in a hollow of the mountain; and that he himself had heard, one summer afternoon, the sound of their balls, like distant peals of thunder.

To make a long story short, the company broke up, and returned to the more important concerns of the election. Rip's daughter took him home to live with her; she had a snug, well-furnished house, and a stout cheery farmer for her husband, whom Rip recollected for one of the urchins that used to climb upon his back. As to Rip's son and heir, who was the ditto of himself seen leaning against the tree, he was employed to work on the farm; but evinced an hereditary disposition to attend to anything else but his business.

Rip now resumed his old walks and habits;

he soon found many of his former cronies, though all rather the worse-for the wear and tear of time; and preferred making friends among the rising generation, with whom he soon grew into great favour.

21.— Having nothing to do at home, and being arrived at that happy age when a man can be idle with impunity, he took his place once more on the bench at the inn door, and was reverenced as one of the patriarchs of the village, and a chronicle of the old times " before the war ". It was some time before he could get into the regular track of gossip, or could be made to comprehend the strange events that had taken place during his torpor. How that there had been a revolutionary war — that the country had thrown off the yoke of old England — and that, instead of being a subject of his Majesty George the Third, he was now a free citizen of the United States. Rip, in fact, was no politician; the changes of states and empires made but little impression on him; but there was one species of despotism under which he had long groaned, and that was — petticoat government. Happily that was at an end; he had got his neck out of the yoke of matrimony, and could go in and out whenever he pleased without dreading the tyranny of Dame Van Winkle. Whenever her name was mentioned, however, he shook his head, shrugged his shoulders, and cast up his eyes; which might pass either for an expression of resignation to his fate, or joy at his deliverance.

He used to tell his story to every stranger that arrived at Mr. Doolittle's hotel. He was observed at first to vary on some points every time he told it, which was, doubtless, owing to his having so recently awaked. It at last settled down precisely to the tale I have related, and not a man, woman, or child in the neighbourhood but knew it by heart. Some always pretended to doubt the reality of it, and insisted that Rip had been out of his head, and that this was one point on which he always remained flighty. The old Dutch inhabitants, however, almost universally gave it full credit. Even to this day they never hear a thunder-storm of a summer afternoon about the Kaatskill, but they say Hendrick Hudson and his crew are at their game of nine-pins; and it is a common wish of all hen-pecked husbands in the neighbourhood, when life hangs heavy on their hands, that they might have a quieting draught out of Rip Van Winkle's flagon.

WASHINGTON IRVING, *le Livre d'esquisses.*

TABLE DES MATIÈRES

Poitiers, Imp. BLAIS, ROY et Cie

www.ingramcontent.com/pod-product-compliance
Lightning Source LLC
LaVergne TN
LVHW021154200726

843510LV00001B/347

9782329675909